The Black Book of Executive Politics
by "Z"

National Institute of Business Management, Inc.
1328 Broadway, New York, NY 10001

About "Z"

You probably know Z. For more than two decades he has helped America's top corporations expand and solidify their companies' leadership roles in highly competitive fields. Noted for his aggressive, opinionated views on business, he has been widely quoted in newspapers and interviewed on radio and television.

Z has agreed to share his secrets for political survival in the corporate arena with the readers of *Executive Strategies*. The sole provision was that his anonymity be preserved.

What follows is a unique, unvarnished collection of political survival tactics from a top corporate executive.

Author	"Z"
Editor	Barry Lenson
Copy Desk Chief	Marie Mularczyk
Editorial Assistant	Teri Zucker
Art Director	John Kwong
Graphics Coordinator	Patricia Spieler
Production Manager	Edmund Leisten
Production Assistant	James Hipkiss
Publisher	Brian W. Smith

The Black Book of Executive Politics

Table of Contents

Table of Contents (cont'd)

3. Survival Skills

Table of Contents (cont'd)

1

What Office Politics Are All About

Introduction

People who fail come in all shapes and sizes. In my years in business, I've seen them all. Some rose through the ranks quickly, only to stall and drop for good like punctured balloons. Some were geniuses who were perennially underappreciated and underrewarded. But most were simply hard-working people with good ideas and instincts—like you, perhaps—who got stuck in permanent ruts and never quite scrambled out to enjoy the light of day.

I've also seen a handful of people who—regardless of education, intelligence, manners, appearance or other obvious factors—have had the knack of rising steadily through the ranks and then *staying on top* through both fat and lean times. They were people who, either consciously or instinctively, knew the art of political survival.

Early in my career I began to watch these people, and I can tell you with certainty what makes them different: The ability to question and discard some, *if not all*, of the rules that snare and finally drown the people they leave in their wake.

What's Holding You Back?

There are hundreds of rules our society tells us to accept blindly and *never* question. Rules so ingrained in most of us since childhood, we don't even feel the crippling limitations they impose on our daily life. Rules such as these:

- Good communication and cooperation gets more work done.

- There are two sides to every question. (Variant: Everybody's entitled to an opinion.)

- Behave consistently if you want other people to respect you.

- Always insist on getting credit for your ideas—and on giving it where it's due.

- To get people to do things for you, you first have to get them to like you.

- The best way to deal with other people is to treat them as you would like to be treated. (Did anybody ever ask you to treat them the way you like to be treated? Sure it's the golden rule, but nine times of out 10 it's just as bad for others as it is for you—or worse.)

- Nonconformity has no place in business—you have to fit in and be a team player.

Do these opinions sound like an inventory of the mental baggage you've been lugging around? If so, good. We've got something to work with.

A Note on Morals

I do not condone immoral or amoral behavior. What I do advocate, however, is *getting things done* by throwing out an overblown, overly polite, crippling world view that keeps most of today's executives tripping over themselves to avoid offending other people. I advocate acting aggressively and effectively—something that, in the end, benefits everyone.

Will you take a chance with me? If I can get you to toss out or just *bend* one or two of the stale, outmoded, useless ideas I'm about to impart in the following pages, I *guarantee* your career will to change in ways you'll hardly believe. If you're ready, here we go.

Your Political Roadmap

Before you can apply the techniques explained in this book, you'll need an organized, clear picture of the lines of power that exist within your workplace.

Start with a sheet of ledger-sized paper and follow these instructions. When done, you'll have a directory of up to 40 people—enough to list all your contacts if you work for a small firm. If you work for a larger company, select the people you'll include based on a roster of your department and allied departments. Include everyone with whom you'll be likely to interact on the job. (A company phone list is a great tool for this purpose.)

Start with the highest-ranking people. Write their names

in a row across the top of the page. Make a circle about two inches in diameter around each name, allowing space for comments. Beneath the top-ranked people, write the names of the people who report to them, and continue down the chart *past* your level so that there is enough room for one or two ranks of names *beneath* you. *Note:* If you have to list more than 25 people, it will be easier to write each name on a separate slip of paper, arrange the slips on the ledger, then copy the names onto the master sheet when you have arranged them according to rank.

Your next step is to write one or two of your impressions and comments about each person in his or her circle. Be sure to include information about the type of relationship you have with each one, interests you share, and potential areas of conflict. Next—and this is the crux of the matter—indicate all reporting relationships by drawing lines between the circles using a blue pen (some of the lines will have to be curved). Using a red pen, draw lines to indicate any *personal* or *strong political* alliances you have perceived between people, which may or may not coincide with reporting lines.

On each line, write one or two facts about the reporting relationship. Use a pencil so you can update information when necessary. *Examples:* John reports to Mary, but only on budget; Sue is too completely dependent on Elaine, and can't make a decision without consulting her.

Don't leave this roadmap lying around—it is a valuable political tool. It allows you to visualize instantly all the relationships and crossrelationships that exist in your workplace, putting you at an instant advantage over people who try to carry around all this information in their head. It gives you a view of the areas where you can exert influence on people. . .often without talking to them directly. It can even help you chart a path to your next promotion or analyze power factions within your support staff.

Don't fail to update your roadmap every two or three days. When you're dealing with a large number of individuals, you'll be surprised how frequently new situations evolve.

You'll be amazed at the power edge this tool will give you. But, after all, that's why you bought this book.

Your Personal Power Inventory

To solidify your position and win advancement in today's competitive business climate, you have to apply all the abilities and assets you have at your disposal. Don't fall into the following patterns that used to be politically effective, but that fall far short of the mark today:

■ **Working harder and harder.** Political advancement does require that you do an excellent job to earn respect. But throwing hard work alone at the problem is not enough.

■ **Relying on a limited support base.** You could build a system made up of a limited group of friends from your college, community, or elsewhere. But using this approach exclusively is too limiting and cuts off more support than it provides.

■ **Trading favors.** The old back scratching *can* win self-advancement. This approach has its usefulness as an isolated technique, but relying on it exclusively turns you into a caricature of an oily schemer.

Your Keys to Power

When thinking politically today, you have to uncover the many tools you possess that you're not using, overcome any resistance you may have to activating them, then apply them aggressively in a structured pattern of getting ahead. Consider the assets you may not be using:

■ **Beliefs and interests.** If you have strong political, moral, spiritual, or other beliefs, don't keep them a secret on the job. Hobbies, sports, and other interests can also gain you an immediate set of connections.

■ **Heritage.** While discriminating *against* people makes you an anachronistic legal liability, don't be reluctant to take advantage of your cultural, religious, racial, or national background when selecting a firm to work for or when building alliances.

■ **Education and schooling.** Look for well-placed alumni of your alma mater. Review what you studied to be sure you are not neglecting skills or interests that could help you rise on the job.

■ **Appearance.** An average appearance shouldn't slow you down in business—but if you're better than average looking, you already stand apart from the crowd. Don't rely on good looks exclusively, but count them as an asset that can help you look the part for a leadership role.

■ **Linguistic ability.** If you grew up speaking a second language or acquired proficiency through study, you have a valuable tool. Use it to build ties to others who speak the same language, and look for opportunities to help your business move into foreign markets or establish ties abroad.

■ **Community.** Do you live in the same community as colleagues or members of upper management? Sharing a commute—or some talk about town politics and other community concerns—can strengthen a valuable alliance.

■ **Home.** If you can use your home to host power parties, why not?

■ **Family.** Don't be reluctant to call upon your relatives for advice or help. And sharing talk with colleagues about children's schooling and other family matters can establish a comfortable common ground with fellow workers. If your spouse can offer advice to your colleagues on various concerns such as real estate, investments, etc., don't be shy about taking advantage of it.

■ **Possessions.** Do you collect paintings, cars, or stamps? Don't hesitate to make these interests known at work—you may find a network of other people who share your interests.

■ **Personality.** You *can* build an alliance based on this elusive factor. Do you have a keen sense of humor? Are you a hard-boiled skeptic or grump? These traits can work for you. Look for people who share your outlook and stop by to laugh about some recent event, or exchange grumpy thoughts.

■ **Style.** Are you a sophisticate, a jock, a chic dresser, a tweedy rumpled type, or something else? You may have to make some stylistic modifications to survive in certain businesses, but look for colleagues who share your approach—you'll experience a higher level of comfort and better communication with these people.

Your Executive Style

In order to advance, you'll need to be taken seriously. Curiously, the most successful people I have known have rarely shared an awful lot of traits, either physical, intellectual, or attitudinal. What, then, is the style that draws leaders upward toward the board room, and how can *you* acquire it?

■ **Individuality.** Don't try to anticipate what other people might like—simply espouse enthusiastically what you *do*. While sharing pursuits with others is important, having an involved, enthusiastic life is what will make you attractive to others—not whether they share all your interests and pursuits.

In an effort to cultivate corporate style, many young managers try to emulate the attitudes, interests, and outlooks of all their colleagues. They try to fit in, and finally do just that—right into pigeonhole-sized niches they built for themselves. *My view:* Trying to conform to corporate culture is a mistake—if your business is inhospitable to your style and way of thinking, trying to conform will only make you a fish out of water. You're in the wrong business.

■ **Standards.** Carefully define what your business and personal principles really are—then stick by them staunchly, no matter how difficult the circumstances. *Example:* If you are fully committed to the profitability of your department and it's time to let some workers go, fire those who are least capable—regardless of your personal feelings. *Central issue:* Do you want to make friends or earn *respect*?

■ **Focus.** The ability to concentrate completely on a task and get it done is central to gaining advancement. And unlike intelligence, this ability can be developed. Focus is also the most important part of what is often called "executive presence." To see it in action, observe the person of power in a meeting. While others are veering off toward other issues, this person will not be dissuaded from his or her goals.

■ **Appropriateness.** Treat serious issues with a serious attitude. While telling a few jokes to blow off steam may break the tension of difficult decisions, it will make you appear uncommitted.

■ **Sobriety.** Nothing will undermine your credibility more quickly than having a few drinks at lunch and returning to the workplace smelling of alcohol. *Even worse:* drinking and acting out of character at a holiday party or picnic. What you do at home is your affair—but what you do at work is your *business.* By the same token, inappropriate romantic or sexual liaisons will push you right off the corporate ladder (see page 38, Sexual Come-Ons in the Office).

How to Tell What a Person Can Do For You: A Tale of Two Executives

The most common mistake people make in deciding which contacts are the most worthwhile is jumping to conclusions—failing to allow enough time to develop a full picture of a contact's strengths and connections. Here's an example:

About 10 years ago, a firm I was working for hired two young marketing executives whose duties, in part, included assuming the workload of an older, semiretired man. One of the young executives immediately dismissed the older man as a has-been and started to propose all sorts of new programs and projects. The other young executive realized that the outgoing man was a virtual gold mine of information and political connections and started using him to establish a broad network of client contacts. Today, the smarter young man is situated near the top of the company's structure. The other guy is right where he started—probably still making dumb snap judgments that block his path to success.

So, if you're wise (and you must be if you're reading this book), pay attention to the following points when deciding which contacts to cultivate and how to use them:

- **Do your homework.** As noted above, the worst mistake is jumping to a premature judgment based on appearance or prejudice. Learn everything you can about a contact's history, both before joining the company and after. If appropriate, simply ask the person about his or her history, activities, and ideas.

  If you're trying to learn about someone who is inaccessible because he or she outranks you, your only means of gaining a picture of his or her influence is to ask everyone you can about what the subject of your inquiry did in the past, and about his or her major accomplishments. Ask about your subject's management style, and about the types of subordinates he or she prefers to work with. Don't forget to ask, too, about education, interests, personal life, etc.

- **Confirm your findings.** In a casual way, confirm your findings with other people. *One technique:* Say to another colleague: "We're really lucky to have Chris here, after she spearheaded the development of that successful line at Plum Software." Watch and listen carefully to gauge your confirming contact's reaction.

- **Hone your observations.** Using the roadmap (see page 3), begin to develop a picture of the person's responsibilities, reporting lines, and activities. As you gather information, enter it into your roadmap. Note projects or programs the person is currently overseeing, or has headed up in the past.

■ **Go outside the firm.** If my hunches are right, the smarter young executive in the example above made some calls and learned that the older man's expertise was highly respected in the field. *Fact:* By going outside your firm, you'll nearly *always* learn things that you can't learn within. For example, if your subject brought an extraordinary amount of success to his or her former employer—a success that your firm has never been able to match—odds are that someone outside your firm will provide more detail about it than a co-worker will.

■ **Consider the person's status and age.** No matter how much a young, fast-moving manager may know, odds are that he or she won't share the information freely with you. The same may be true for a middle ager. It is a truism—but often true nonetheless—that older managers are the most likely to be forthcoming with help, ideas, and political assistance for people with the meat of their career still ahead of them. You can cultivate the support of younger managers, but it will usually take more time to achieve the same advantageous position that comes more easily with many older colleagues.

Political Mistakes from Which You Will Never Recover

Now that you're on your way toward building a bullet-proof political network, it's time to give you a list of things you should *never* do. An unfortunate byproduct of political structures is that they will network *against* you as well as *for* you if word gets out that you've made a blunder.

Be especially careful of the following political gaffes:

■ **Bad timing.** Before asking someone for help, consider whether your relationship is ready to bear the weight of what you are requesting. *Example:* If you haven't progressed beyond establishing that you and your contact share an interest in travel, it's too soon to ask for help in winning a new sales territory.

■ **Toe Stepping.** Before you look to people for support, consider the positions they occupy. *Example:* If a new territory or set of responsibilities is up for grabs, asking the head of another department for help in winning them may be a serious misplay if he or she is considering making a play for them also. *Exception:* If your alliance with them is exceptionally strong and well maintained, asking for support can result in their dropping out of the competition, sometimes without resentment. Alternatively, it may open up discussion of a mutually beneficial approach to the problem.

■ **Relying on foundationless alliances.** If you're friendly and cordial with another manager, that's not enough to enable you to rely on him or her for strong support. Be sure that there is a variety of other supporting factors—and a history of cooperation—to add a foundation to your relationship.

■ **Overusing an alliance.** The more valuable an alliance, the *less* often you should use it for help with big projects. (*Note:* A strong ally will be working silently for your interests in many small ways without your knowing it every day.) If you walk into a highly placed colleague's office too often to ask for a big favor, the quality of your connection will erode quickly. *Analogy:* Think of an alliance as a rechargeable battery—after using it, you have to reenergize it before tapping into it again. After getting a favor, return a favor in a big way, or do some high-level stroking to keep the alliance running strong.

■ **Posturing.** When trying to win support or influence someone, it is *very dangerous* to infer that your project should be supported because you are strongly connected to someone at the top. First, the inference is a threat. Second, if the top person turns out to be a less-than-staunch supporter in this instance, you're going to lose face with everyone. Third, everyone will know that you are strongly connected to the bigwig anyway, and will weigh that information in deciding whether or not to support you. Blowing your own horn only makes you a blowhard.

■ **Letting alliances lapse.** If the very person who can help you is someone with whom you used to enjoy close political ties—but you've been neglecting him or her lately—it's a serious blunder to count on picking up your former close relationship where it left off. It is also a serious misplay to start currying favor suddenly by taking the person out to lunch, calling him or her up to chat, etc., before making a pitch for support. *Best:* Maintain close ties to your colleagues, letting none of them lapse. *Next best:* Come clean. Tell the person that you are aware you haven't been in close touch lately, but that you have good memories of the projects you've shared in the past, and that you are calling to ask for support. Strengthen this approach with an immediate offer of support for one of your contact's current concerns.

2

The Influence Game

How to Tell How Much Clout an Opponent *Really* Has

All of us have gotten into neck-and-neck races with another department head or executive. It can be as elemental as a two-person fight for one promotion slot, or as complicated as a political struggle to increase staffing during crunch times.

In direct competition, you are comparing yourself to your adversary: your work records, length of employment, a lot of things. But beyond all these variables—and the sum total of them all—is the elusive factor known as *clout*.

Roughly defined, it is the degree of acceptance that upper management has accorded you—versus other people—based on your past efforts, personality, and political strength. No two employees have the same clout. It's one of the most important factors in determining who will succeed in a life-or-death struggle.

Clout vs. Posturing

An insecure opponent will usually resort to posturing: alluding to connections, dropping names, and bragging about how much he or she has contributed to the firm in the past. Alternately, a close political ally of your opponent may drop by to convey this information to you indirectly.

If your adversary throws up this smoke cloud, don't be discouraged. He or she *may* actually be in a position of power. You won't know until you confirm the following information. Don't be intimidated prematurely or you may lose the fight.

- *Activity.* Is this person still on the same committees that he or she served on two or three years ago?

- *Connections.* What personnel changes have occurred *above* the person? Did he or she lose an umbrella of support when a close supervisor left?

- *Staff.* How many people does this person supervise? Has this number gone up or down over the last year? Over the last two years? Why did the people leave?

- *Positioning.* Where is your company heading? Considering current company policy and plans, compare the role of your department to that of your adversary. For example, a head of marketing may have an advantage over a head of sales in a firm that is moving away from field sales and into direct marketing promotions.

- *Personality.* If you find your opponent unpleasant, odds are that upper management does too. Unless they need an ogre to do the job, you are probably at an advantage.

Fighting Intimidation: How to Spot Deceitful People

It's great to solidify your power and build your political network. The downside is that you are going to become the target of carping from envious—and often malicious—people who will try to intimidate you, bruise your self-image, and make you feel your growing power is of no significance.

Your best strategy—the only one, really, if you're going to win—is to study power plays with objectivity and learn as much as you can. The wonderful truth is that they offer you the chance to learn a tremendous amount about your enemies and opponents—far more than you could if they were silently dreaming up plots against you. They're making the mistakes, and you're reaping the benefits.

Here are the most common types of detractors, and what you can do about them:

■ **Self-aggrandizers.** These opponents routinely exaggerate accomplishments or political clout. When the company president says good morning to them in the hall, they come by to tell you they just had a policy meeting. *Key:* Over a period of time, look objectively for discrepancies between what a person says and what you see is happening. Perennial self-aggrandizers are generally not taken seriously by anyone. Unless there are some mitigating factors (the posturer is the president's nephew, for example), you need not take them too seriously either.

- **Insinuators.** They engage in Iago-like intrigue. *Example:* Your opponent stops by to tell you that the controller had to rewrite your quarterly earnings report because it was disorganized. A *real* snake may even infer that he or she is on your side and offer to help you complete projects to avoid further trouble. *Defense:* Confirm any reports directly with all those concerned. Insinuators *are* dangerous because they'll take their intrigue on to other people after they have failed with you—they are also often highly magnetic people who gain credibility with other people for awhile. Your best defense is to wait until this type of person plays the same card too often and is exposed for what he or she is. *Mistake:* Warning another employee that the insinuator is a chronic liar can drag you into a morass of charges and countercharges.

- **Sleight-of-hand artists.** This type tries to throw you off by providing some spurious information. *Example:* Just before a meeting, he or she will tell you: "That idea of yours will never get approved—the vice-president proposed the same thing last year and it got shot down." *Defense:* It's hard not to be fooled once or twice by this type—especially if he or she is clever—but make sure you're not fooled from then on.

- **Strategists.** When you're cooperating on a project with this type, he or she says there's no pressure and starts off at a sluggish pace. When you follow the lead and start slowly, he or she secretly catapults forward, finishes far ahead of you, then turns in his or her work early to make you look like a snail. *Defense:* Do your work at your own pace, and don't be intimidated. Just because the strategist thinks he or she is earning points with upper management by these antics doesn't mean it is the case.

■ **Bullies.** People who try to bulldoze or intimidate you are hard to analyze. Your best defense is to assess their clout objectively (see page 16, How to Tell How Much Clout an Opponent *Really* Has), and firmly stand your ground despite all attempts to sway you.

Gaining an Advantage

The bottom line is that you must understand what motivates these forms of aggression—and formulate appropriate defense strategies. It is almost *never* productive to retaliate in kind. You'll gain more by understanding the behavior, anticipating its repeated use, and turning that knowledge to your advantage.

Times When It Is Necessary to Use Your Clout

The greatest enemy you can have in the workplace is a false sense of comfort. It makes you numb to warning signs that some setback is being planned for you, and also blinds you to potential opportunities for future advancement. You're at most risk—and most in need of political support—at the following times:

■ **The risky project.** Lending your support to a new project can advance your position, or deal you a real setback if the project bombs. Be selective about the projects you back. It's better to be remembered for three remarkable successes than for four remarkable successes and one or two failures.

■ **Reduced responsibilities.** If your company changes direction and your responsibilities change, find out fast what your new role will be. *Fact:* A temporary cutback in responsibilities usually turns into a permanent downturn in your firm's need for you.

■ **Increased responsibilities.** Taking on an additional workload or department can be a boon for your career, but make sure the job is manageable and that the work suits your abilities. Find out as much as you can about who did the job before, why he or she is not doing it any longer, and what the company goals are for the new department or projects. *Key:* Avoid mismatches. If the new duties are allied to what you're already doing, odds are that you'll be able to handle them. But if management is dumping something on you just because you're perceived as capable, watch out. *Example:* A sales manager I knew was asked to assume responsibility for customer fulfillment. Even though fulfillment was a small department in the firm, the job was so different from his sales duties that he had to continuously shift mental gears. Worst of all, the physical layout required that he have two separate offices *on different floors.* He spent half his time returning phone calls he had missed.

■ **You're catapulted up.** Management loves you and wants

to offer you a crack at *real* responsibility and accountability. *Variation:* A very risky, high-visibility project. Opportunity has knocked, but be sure that your skills and contacts will support you. You don't want to be a victim of a "Let's see if young McCarthy can handle this" experiment.

■ **You're making a fortune.** You've moved ahead, have been in the same job for a number of years, and there are other executives eager to do your job for half the money you're making. Unless your political connections are rock solid—and almost nobody's are—your best plan is to move either up or out before you've spent more than two or three years on your lofty perch.

■ **A change of location.** Before you take a job in a branch office, make sure that it's not a trip to nowhere. *Example:* I know a man who, two years before retirement, was offered a job to direct the Canadian division of an American-based firm. He called some contacts outside the firm and learned of a strong rumor that the division was about to be closed. He refused the post, and the division *did* close within the year.

■ **You're stalling.** You're not at the top, but your upward progress has stopped. *Warning signs:* You're not included in meetings or invited to join newly formed committees. Your staff is being reduced. You're getting positive feedback on job reviews, but no promotions. If you're being glad-handed, odds are that a knife is being sharpened for your back. It's time for some fence mending. You may even have to leave if you've allowed your support network to erode.

- You've got a new boss. To avoid landing back at the starting line, learn as much as you can about the new person. Early on, try to find some common political ground with the new supervisor and make an assessment of his or her managerial style.

The Story of Mr. O— The Incredible Power of Opinion

Of all the commonly held, stale misconceptions in our society, one of the most damaging is the idea that there are two valid sides to every issue. We're all supposed to believe that other people's views are just as valid as ours, and that they deserve equal consideration.

This hidden rule impedes progress. How many times have you been in a meeting that generated no ideas because everyone was trying to be open to everyone else or—at best—proposing lukewarm solutions to avoid offending anyone?

Enter Mr. O

One of the most remarkable and effective executives I've had the opportunity to observe at close working range owed much of his success to breaking this rule. For our purposes here, let's call him Mr. O. Having started as head of a branch office, he had been promoted to director of operations for an electronics company in just a few short years. When I collaborated with him, Mr. O had remained on top for nearly a decade, solidifying his position at the same time as he guided his growing company to a position of prominence in its field.

Mr. O was not a visionary genius. He was hardly ever armed with some polished, fully formed idea. But what he *did* have—every single time—was an *opinion*.

In fact, the ability to be opinionated was really the only thing that set him aside from his colleagues. He would stride into a meeting armed with some idea or plan he believed was irrefutably brilliant, and everyone present would be forced to either react positively, or propose—and defend—another approach to the problem.

Plans were made, and projects completed effectively, simply because Mr. O's opinions acted like a fulcrum for other people to use in their thinking and work. I observed that ideas from almost everyone on the staff were being implemented—not just the ones from this man. Yet he was the reason for the firm's progress. And it was *he* who got the credit, a salary well into six figures, and his picture in glossy business magazines.

How to Double Your Chances of Getting Others to See Things Your Way—A Checklist for Negotiators

The more you want something you're about to negotiate for, the more you're likely to weaken your chances by overpreparing and overdocumenting your case.

You're far more likely to win if you make *smart* preparations rather than *hard* preparations. Review the following checklist:

■ **Keep things simple.** Distill your ideas into a few sentences, and keep supporting paperwork minimal for the negotiating session itself.

■ **Structure your presentation.** Reveal your biggest idea immediately, without preambles. *Example:* Don't say "I have a proposal so far-reaching I predict it will make $2 million this year alone." Just present your idea clearly and let predictions follow. If your first points are well received, go on to make your second and third points—but resist the temptation to keep throwing in lesser and lesser points—they only weaken your stance.

■ **Anticipate objections.** Be sure to do your homework on how management is likely to react to your proposal. Research how it has treated similar proposals in the past, and anticipate objections your opponents are likely to make.

■ **Build in some sacrifices.** To protect the meat of your proposal—the things you really don't want to see cut out—add a few chips you're willing to give up. You can then bargain them away and end up with the parts that mean the most to you.

■ **Don't try to score all the points.** Your position will actually be strengthened—and cooperation much more likely—if you accede to some ideas from people who are critiquing your presentation.

■ **Meet resistance flexibly.** When you care a great deal about a project, you may tend to overreact when anybody raises questions. *Best:* Treat objections with humor, and try to foster an atmosphere of cooperation—it implies that your project is already underway. If negotiations stall completely, try to ascertain what aspect of your proposal is *really* bothering the other side. Don't become argumentative, but try to read between the lines of what is being said. As a last resort, consider throwing one of your sacrifice chips away to get things moving.

■ **Don't give away the store.** Accept a certain number of modifications to your plan or idea, but don't let it get converted into another person's project that you're now expected to supervise. If you see this happening, offer to withdraw the entire proposal for further development.

■ **Rise above politics.** It's funny advice to be giving in this book, but try not to consider whom your opponents are when you're actually making a presentation—even if they are right there in the room. The more important your proposal, the more vital it is to appear to have the interests of the entire company at heart—especially when top management is in attendance. Don't betray any aggressive feelings toward your opponents or act condescending toward them—even if you think they are stupid, and even if they are.

How to Take Intelligent Risks That Lead You Upward

Your career will never get anywhere unless you are willing to stick your neck out periodically and try something truly risky. This shows that you have vision and courage. But being the driving force behind a number of unsuccessful projects won't win you any points with anyone, and can quickly deflate your self-esteem. Before taking on the risk, assess the dangers:

■ **What are the worst—and best—things that can happen?** *Example:* If the worst thing that can happen is that you'll irritate your staff, and the best thing is that you'll contribute significantly to the bottom line, the risk is worthwhile.

■ **Do I have the total support of the people I need?** Look at your political roadmap (see page 3, Your Political Roadmap) and consider whom you will need to support you. If necessary, reinforce your critical political alliances.

■ **Is it fun?** If you can convince yourself, your staff, and your superiors that the task is challenging and fun, you're far more likely to gain needed support. *Ploy:* Frame the undertaking in an appealing way to gain support—similar to Tom Sawyer whitewashing Aunt Polly's fence.

■ **What are the implications for my career path?** If you undertake a risky assignment and succeed, you become strongly associated with what you have done—a tie that will exert a force on what people ask you to do in the future. Consider the implications before acting.

■ **What are the theatrical possibilities?** Don't take on

risk silently. Consider ways to frame it in such a way that it builds your visibility and reputation.

The Solitary Risk

When the time comes to take on something risky all alone—going to the president to complain about your supervisor or to ask for a chance to lead a new division—you are in a sacrificial situation: You're ready to take on great risk on the chance that you'll win out. Follow these steps:

■ **Understand and minimize the risk.** Have a concrete plan for what you'll do if you lose. *Example:* If your complaints about your boss fall on deaf ears, your only recourse may be to leave the firm. Check your financial resources and chances for employment elsewhere. *Ask:* Am I really desperate enough to take these risks now, or should I wait until I am in a stronger position?

■ **Analyze the outcome if you succeed.** Are you ready to deal with what you've taken on? *Trap:* Romanticizing the joy of how wonderful it will be to advance yourself rapidly by taking a big chance. It *can* be wonderful—but the wise risk taker knows what he or she is getting into well before it's a done deal.

■ **Prepare.** Don't just reinforce your key political connections two or three days before you make your move. If you're playing with this degree of risk, you had better keep your fences mended—and reinforced—at all times.

3

Survival Skills

How to Negotiate When Someone Stonewalls

Negotiating is supposed to be a two-way street. But what do you do when your opponent takes a stance, stands pat, and refuses to even discuss your ideas? Making more suggestions doesn't accomplish anything because it's off limits according to the ground rules that you didn't create. In extreme cases, this ploy may be accompanied by personal attacks against you or your intelligence.

If you're getting tied up, try these tactics:

- **Don't avoid silence.** When an aggressive person has stated his or her main point vehemently, remain silent. The person will feel foolish about repeating it. The next thing the critic says will almost inevitably involve a softening of his or her position.

- **Don't go on the offensive.** Attacking your opponent's ideas is exactly what he or she hopes you will do—it locks you into fighting in his or her arena rather than yours. Sidestep the attack. Try to understand the principles on which the ideas are based and use them to further your own aims. *Why this works:* Instead of opposing force with force, you're using your opponent's own strength to further your own ideas.

■ **Divert the aggression.** Unless you can profit from the confrontation, try to subvert any attacks on you into attacks on the problem. You can get angry too, and maybe further your own ends by joining your attacker. You can agree that your ideas need work, and invite your opponent to offer some suggestions.

Listen to suggestions but, more importantly, try to discern an underlying pattern of what they are trying to accomplish by opposing you.

When Teamwork *Isn't* the Answer

Cooperation is great, but it isn't always the best way to get things done. There are times when everyone must pull in the same direction toward a common goal—and other times when you can use divisiveness as a motivational factor.

Before you set people one against another, consider the following:

■ **The nature of the project.** If you're engaged in a high-visibility project, don't discourage teamwork. People will say: "Look at what they were able to accomplish despite terrible managerial input." If, on the other hand, your main concern is getting *results* fast in an undertaking that won't be under public scrutiny, your project may be ripe for discord.

■ **The personalities involved.** Most of the people involved—especially those who are most expert or doing most of the work—must be sturdy types who can deal with some unpleasantness and conflict. But if key players are easily bruised, you had better go the route of cooperation.

■ **The political structure of the group.** If everybody is closely allied, creating internal discord will be difficult—and possibly harmful in the long run. *Best:* In such instances, make the competition overt by dividing the group into teams and offering incentives to the team that gets the best work done the soonest.

Taking Advantage of Discord

If political divisiveness is already present within the group, do a quick analysis of who belongs to what camp, and where each member's influence is strongest. Divide duties up so that people do things they are best suited to do—and for which they have the best political connections.

Fostering an atmosphere of competition among your subordinates can be highly beneficial. By setting high expectations and standards, and letting subordinates compete to win your approval, you'll get more work done. And, quite possibly, bring out the best in everyone.

Remember that the approaches that seem to be kindest

are not necessarily the ones that enable people to reach their highest potential within an organization.

The Power of Acting Out of Character—And How Not to Become a Victim of It

Consciously acting out of character is manipulative, but it is one of the most powerful tools at your disposal.

On at least one important occasion, it worked for me. In my first job after college, I was called into the office of one of the company vice-presidents—a man who was, to put it mildly, aloof. In fact, he had not even nodded at me up until that moment. When I entered his office, he invited me to sit, and was very cordial. He asked a lot of questions about my college studies (a good place to hit me because I still felt like a college kid at the time), my interests, my family, and whether I had found satisfactory living quarters. He then outlined some stiff responsibilities he wanted me to assume, and I left his office. The next day, all I could get from him was a hurried nod in the hall again, but I was already off and running.

I was manipulated by a change of style on this occasion—but the ruse was as beneficial for me as it was for the manipulator: I got extra motivation to get the work done—and that contributed toward my advancement.

Note that this story bears out one of the central ideas of this book: Bending the rules gets things done, and, in most cases, helps everyone out.

Using Technique

In order to act out of character, it is necessary to define what your character generally is. And it's equally important to use this technique only occasionally, especially with people at your own level or with superiors. You may get away with it more often with people you supervise, but remember that continually shifting your stance waters down your personality rather than giving it strength.

Here are some basic character polarities, and how to use them:

- **Familiarity vs. Aloofness.** As in the example above, sudden friendliness achieves results. If you are habitually gregarious, on the other hand, a dose of aloofness can go a long way toward making people think you have something on your mind or that they are not performing to your satisfaction.

- **Politeness vs. Brusqueness.** If you're a cut-the-crap type, a sudden act of politeness (holding the door for a colleague or helping someone into his or her overcoat) can temporarily disarm an opponent or predispose an ally toward doing a favor for you. If, on the other hand, you are a model of civility and decorum, storming out of a meeting *once* in your career is probably a good idea.

- **Seriousness vs. Humor.** Shifting from one pole to the other can produce stirring results. If you're a never-crack-a-smile type, you can sway a meeting *once* every two or three years by opening the session with some cornball or off-color joke. On the other hand, if you have a sunny personality most of the time, you can put some steel in people's spines by *refraining* from laughing when everyone else does.

■ **Opinionatedness vs. Passiveness.** If you always state your views strongly, you can motivate a colleague by saying: "You're in charge on this project, Chris—I trust you to do what is necessary." On the other hand, if you're more passive in nature, try taking a superstrong line or setting a strict deadline for an important project.

Fighting Manipulation from Others

Either consciously or unconsciously, other people will try to use the techniques similar to those outlined above to manipulate *you*. To avoid being pushed and pulled around, observe people closely and try to determine patterns of behavior. When their way of relating to you or to other people changes abruptly, consider the context. Chances are that you'll be able to read their purposes more clearly than you might expect.

Another important tool is to keep a steady course. Prioritize your own activities according to your goals and needs, and remain steady. By showing that you're incapable of being manipulated off your course, you will force people to deal with you on a more honest plane.

To get you to do what they want, they'll have to come to you, speak honestly about their desires, and ask for your cooperation.

How to Reprimand a Subordinate

T he classic rules of reprimanding a subordinate have always been to do it behind closed doors and to avoid personal attack. They're good ones. Bend them only when the employee is a repeat offender you're trying to embarrass or motivate to quit, or when there are other special circumstances.

Preparation is the key to effective reprimands. Arm yourself with appropriate documentation for the points you wish to make. Otherwise you'll have to stop in midstream and resume later when you have your information together. That's awkward and it gives your subordinate time to think up a defense.

Presenting Your Case

Here's how to capitalize on your position of strength:

■ **Wait until you're under control.** While you may gain an edge by issuing a reprimand while you're angry, it can also work against you because you're more likely to forget to make key points or think clearly about solutions to the problem. If you want to appear angry, act angry— but wait until you are really calm internally and in control.

■ **Be specific about the offense.** Make your complaints one at a time. Don't try to soften any blows—be straightforward.

■ **Give the person a chance to issue an explanation.**

There may be extenuating circumstances, but it's more likely that the employee will simply own up to the problem and start suggesting ways to improve.

■ **Don't harbor a grudge.** Unless the employee is an habitual offender, say that the book is closed on the issue—provided that the situation will change. If it does not, the fact that you've treated the employee fairly and seen no improvement only serves to add to your clout the next time you issue a reprimand or move to have the offender terminated.

How to Manipulate Without Alienating

There *are* times when you want to alienate people, but other times you want them to do what you say without causing permanent resentment or hatred. *Here are the tools you need to perform this delicate surgery—cutting out the bad feelings while leaving the good:*

■ **Inspire sympathy.** Let the person know that he or she will bear some of the responsibility for what will happen to you if he or she doesn't do what you want done. *Say:* "Our department's profits will drop by four percent again this month if you don't get your customer to pay that bill, and I'm in enough trouble already."

■ **Ask for a favor to be returned.** *Say:* "Remember I helped push through the budgeting for that new equipment of yours last quarter? Well, I need you to return the favor now."

■ **Make your request part of a current project.** If you can imply that the favor you're requesting is something the person has already agreed to undertake, the effect of your asking for it may be softened. *Say:* "Those preliminary numbers in your sales report looked fine. How will the receipt of monies from your Cincinnati clients add to it?"

■ **Make your request an exception to the rule.** *Say:* "As you know, I hardly ever have to ask anybody to do something in such strong terms, but it is absolutely imperative that you fire Johnson immediately."

■ **Allude to authority.** *Say:* "Top management is demanding that we give them those figures by Friday. Do whatever is necessary to get the work done." This transfers some of the onus onto top management. For this technique to work, there must be truth in your allegation: If your subordinate finds out that all the top managers will be starting their weekend early by taking Friday off, you have made a serious blunder.

■ **Offer support.** *Say:* "This is a top priority. Can I get someone else to help you?" *Fact:* Most of the time a person will turn down your offer to provide help because he or she wants to show you that the is situation under control.

■ **Flatter the person.** Don't pull this card out of the deck very often, or people will brand you as insincere. And always offer flattery that is based on *truth*—you don't want to praise the appearance of the office slob. As a once-in-a-blue-moon tactic, few influencing techniques can approach this classic ploy's effectiveness. *Say:* "Nobody around here has as much tact with people as you do. How about applying those people skills of yours to getting that bill paid?"

Sexual Come-Ons in the Office and What to Do About Them

The current efforts to safeguard all employees against the pressure of sexual harassment on the job are laudable and long overdue. However, it is important to remember that sexual attractions are a natural part of the chemistry that grows when a group of people gather—and the workplace is certainly not exempt.

■ Sometimes, that most wonderful of all situations arises on the job—you meet Ms. or Mr. Right, fall head over heels, and the two of you plan to spend the rest of your lives together. When this happens, the rest of the issues have a way of sorting themselves out—when and how to tell co-workers, and whether one of you should leave the firm in order to preserve a healthy business and domestic relationship.

But other sexual interactions pose more questions. When someone makes a sexual overture toward you, you had better answer the following questions:

■ **Is it a power play?** Since Biblical times, people have been using sex—either promised or provided—to advance themselves. Look at the person's position objectively and decide whether he or she may need your support for some political end.
Then look at your own emotions: If you feel terribly complimented, empowered, or excited by the sexual advance, take care that your own emotions don't lead you into a trap.

■ **Is it just sleazy?** Men and women who are bored and looking for sexual liaisons among co-workers have failed to assess their professional or personal priorities. Avoid them.

■ **Is it interesting?** It would be crazy to tell people never to enter into relationships with any co-workers. If you have determined (after waiting a reasonable amount of time and doing some reflecting) that the personal and political risks are minimal, you may decide to make an informed decision to explore the attraction—but always do it outside the workplace. However, be aware that there are always more risks than you can anticipate when romance and work are combined.

■ **What is the context?** If a co-worker invites you to dinner or the theater, the flirtation has begun on a fairly sophisticated plane and is mutually agreed upon. However, a sudden advance at the office party—allowing no time for you to consider the ramifications—should be rebuffed at all costs. It can easily make you the center of gossip and destroy the credibility it may have taken you years to achieve.

How to Handle the Press Like a Pro

Frankly, I couldn't tell you how to attract positive publicity for your firm. You'd better talk to a public relations expert about that. But what I *can* tell you about is how to handle a hostile press when you're under fire for something your firm has—or has not—done.

First, do yourself the favor of claiming some basic privileges for yourself: the right to be treated politely and fairly; the right to have a chance to say what you want to; and the right to remain in control of the situation—including the right to turn your back and walk out of the room if your other rights are not being respected.

Coping with Emergencies

With luck, you'll have time to assess the situation and gather background information before you're on the spot. However—an executive's nightmare—there may come a time when you're suddenly before the cameras trying to explain why your company's oil tank caught fire, or why your firm is closing a plant that employed a large number of people.

The *worst* thing you can do is lie to the press about what happened. Just as harmful is to issue an opinion based on skimpy information in the hope that you'll later be proven right by the facts.

■ The press certainly won't want to hear the "That matter

is currently under investigation" line. But in reality, it is often the safest and most honest thing you can say.

But honesty will only get you so far with reporters, who may try to trip you up with the following ploys:

- **The "What if. . .?" question.** *Example:* "What if the fire spreads and fatalities result—will your firm make restitution to the families of victims?" Don't ever let yourself get pulled into speculation. Reporters can trap you in a seemingly unimportant one, and then lead you into more damaging statements.

- **The "yes or no" question.** *Example:* "Did your company take adequate safety precautions? Yes or no?" This is an overt ploy to make you look bad, and it will work. To limit the damage, say: "We will be issuing a report containing that information shortly," but don't pick some arbitrary date when an answer will be forthcoming.

- **The "number one priority" question.** *Example:* "What is your company's number one priority in fighting pollution?" If you say you're reducing your plant's output of airborne pollutants, the press might criticize you for ignoring water-purity restrictions. *Defense:* Say "We are attacking many major concerns, including. . ."

- **The "off the record" question.** Always respond to a reporter as though your statements will become a matter of public record. Odds are that they will.

- **The "either/or" question.** *Example:* "Either your company wants to keep the citizens of this town employed, or it wants to close down the factory. Which is it?" This is an attempt to paint you into a corner. Your best defense is to point out that the "either/or" case is spurious. Time permitting, make an explanation of issues that confront your company at the time.

■ **The "multiple choice" question.** *Example:* "Will you replace outmoded equipment to meet new EPA guidelines, repair the old equipment, or just shut down temporarily?" Simply because the reporter is supplying the options doesn't mean that you can't ignore them and supply some of your own.

■ **The "statement" question.** *Example:* "You obviously don't want to spend money on community development projects." *Defense:* Convert the statement into a question: "If you're asking about our current programs, let me explain them for you. . ."

■ **The "second guess" question.** *Example:* "How do you think your competitors will respond to your new product line?" *Defense:* "You'd better ask *them* that question."

■ **The "policy statement" question.** This can occur when you go before the press armed with information on a specific issue, and then some reporter asks: "What is your company's stand on the environment?" *Defense:* To avoid a lengthy silence or an ill-conceived reply, tie your answer into the matter you came prepared to discuss, and point to it as an example of your company's outlook. Questions like that present a golden opportunity to display your background research, and tell of past activities that show your firm in a positive way.

How to Report Bad News Positively

Problem: How do you give bad news—such as announcing a wage freeze or layoffs—and still have people believe in your personal worth and good intentions? To boost your odds for success:

- *Avoid surprises.* Keep people informed ahead of time that budgetary or other problems are a major management concern.

- *Avoid mixed messages.* Give the bad news and don't try to soften it. Telling people that they're being let go but that the company will now turn a profit will not earn you any points with anyone.

- *Give full information.* While you want to keep your central theme clear and understandable, don't fail to offer as much backup information as you can.

- *Encourage free communication.* Saying: "My door is always open," after you let 10 people go, may make *you* feel better—but probably won't do the same for anyone else. *Better:* Schedule individual appointments with any concerned employees and take care to address their personal concerns and needs. Don't just recite the same speech to each of them.

  If appropriate, have an outplacement or other support system in place and ready to go before delivering bad news.

- *Don't overstate your sorrow.* Even though you may *feel* as badly as the people who are getting the bad news, telling them that you're as miserable as they are will never ring true.

The Pros and Cons of Hiring a Friend

If you have decided that hiring a friend is always either a very good or a bad idea, you haven't given the matter enough thought.

The bottom line is that by hiring someone—whether a friend or a stranger—you are establishing a *professional* relationship. When considering a friend, consider the same factors you would when making any hiring decision—but add the pluses and minuses that your friendship might bring to the professional relationship.

- **Consider your friend objectively.** Are you sure that he or she is *really* the best person for the job? How about other candidates? If your friend is not the most knowledgeable or experienced for the job, do strength of character or the advantages of your relationship outweigh any shortcomings?

- **Consider the nature of your friendship.** Look at areas in which you communicate well, but also consider areas of friction. It's reasonable to expect your professional relationship to mirror these tendencies. *Bottom line:* Preventing problems *before* you hire someone can avoid both professional and personal friction.

■ **Build in an escape chute.** Establish a mechanism for terminating the business relationship if it is not working out, and for regularly sharing views of how the liaison is going. If possible (in a single proprietor or family-run business, for example) it may be desirable to bring your friend in on a temporary basis for a predetermined period of weeks or months, and then cement the relationship if it is working out well.

■ **Consider the benefits—and detriments—of having a friend on the job.** Knowing that you can count on someone can be a tremendous plus. However, it can also cause friction with other staff members who will resent the fact that a colleague has a close personal relationship with you.

■ **Weigh the political implications.** Like it or not, you'll be operating as a team—at least in the public view. Consider the ramifications in the light of the political relationships you've already established. Is hiring your friend worth the potential damage it may cause?

How to Deal Diplomatically with an Opponent Who Steps on Your Toes—And Then Get Even If You Have to

When a colleague has stolen a big idea, spread rumors to undermine your credibility, bad-mouthed your managerial skills to your subordinates, or engaged in some other form of back stabbing, the following strategies will help you reassert your position of power:

■ **Understand what happened.** Rumors may have blown your opponent's act out of proportion. Before doing anything, speak to one or two people to help you draw a bead on what actually occurred. Nothing makes you look more foolish than seriously overreacting to a minor infraction. Don't kill a mosquito with a shotgun.

■ **Act quickly.** Waiting a few days to get your defenses in place only allows the damage to increase.

■ **Respond appropriately.** If another manager has told a member of your staff that you are a bad manager, don't go right to his or her staff and make the same charges—it will only show that you operate on the same low plane as your opponent. Retaliate by winning a bigger victory elsewhere. Consider what your political network can do to help you. *Examples:* Win a key project, or get a subordinate promoted over one of your opponent's. If worse comes to worse, use your circle of influence to put one of your opponent's projects at a disadvantage. At this level, however, you're dealing with an open conflict. The damage may be hard to contain.

■ **Keep your composure.** Don't become erratic. If you're going to become unpleasant or combative, let it be a conscious decision, used to obtain specific results. A calm exterior, coupled with decisive action, lets you come out looking like a pro.

■ **Deal with the problem directly.** Sometimes, it is best

to go directly to the offender to ask exactly what he or she has done, and to demand an explanation. This approach *is* a sacrificial move, and may trigger a feud that will be hard to contain. More often, however, the result is something unexpected—your opponent comes back at you with a countercharge about some offense you committed in the past and have forgotten. If so, you have been handed a bargaining chip. Agree to undo the damage, and it may be possible to arrange a compromise and win the conflict.

As in all other things, a well-maintained political network increases your odds of success—your opponent knows that what happens will affect his or her political fortunes as well as yours.

Getting Out: Knowing When to Take the Money and Run

Whether you should retire, and when, is largely dependent on your personal financial picture. Hopefully, you will have planned, saved, and built such a good program of retirement benefits throughout your career that you can make the decision based on your desires and preferences, rather than financial need.

Assuming that this is the case, you should weigh the following factors before deciding to take early retirement:

- **How much more will your benefits grow if you stick it out until the end?** You may have to ask for help from your accountant or financial planner to determine this. Pay special attention to what amount you have vested in your pension, and how your taxes, social security (if applicable), and other income-providing vehicles will be affected if you bail out early. Also, consider the impact of early retirement on your eventual estate. The bottom line: Over the next 10 years, exactly how much of a difference in income will you experience if you get out now? Over the next 20 years? *Note: If your political alliances are strong, you can have your cake and eat it too by arranging to work on a reduced schedule while increasing pension vesting and eventual social security benefits.*

■ **Do I want to start a new business?** If you're anxious to start one, the chance to do it with a steady income behind you can put you at a considerable advantage over your competition.

■ **Have I completed my work?** If you've reached your career goals, and are in danger of becoming a lame duck, sitting pat won't do you *or* your reputation any good. On the other hand, if your long-term aims are about to be realized, staying at the helm and seeing them through may solidify your reputation, and pave the way for future success.

■ **Where is the business headed?** Look beyond the bottom line. Analyze where profits have come from over the past few years, and where they are likely to come from in the future. Take a good look at what is happening in your industry—and market segment. *Example:* If your products are about to come under stiff competition from a variety of low-priced foreign imports, consider whether it will be enjoyable and challenging for you to suit up and wade into the battle at this point in your career. It could be time to turn the reins of power over to others.

■ **What will I do?** A common mistake is painting a hazy, unfocused picture of how good it will be to have lots of leisure time after retiring. Don't forget that spending more time at home (if that's your plan) will be a major adjustment for your family as well as for you. Try to build a well-defined picture of what you would like to do. Then plan how to do it—whether you will need to move, pursue a second career, etc.

Having a plan in place is critical. A problem I've observed in my friends: A miserable, disquieting first two or three months of retirement can be more than just a tough adjustment period—it can be a profoundly unsettling experience that destroys the joy of retirement.

The Dangerous Game: Bypassing Your Boss

If you fail to get your boss to act on something you propose, it is nearly always a serious blunder to make the same request to upper management. However, there are times when making an end run around your boss may be your only viable option. Here are two examples:

• Your boss can't delegate, let alone act effectively with his or her own supervisors. If he or she isn't pulling for your ideas with upper management, consider suggesting that you pitch one of your own projects directly to the bigwigs. Chances are that your namby-pamby boss will be relieved.

- Your boss has all but pushed you out the door already. Be ready to make the sacrifice and pack up and leave if your play doesn't work. *Example:* Your boss keeps stalling about approaching upper management to request your overdue raise. You're *already* about to quit—so why not go to upper management and ask for a raise *and* a transfer to another department? *Danger:* If you get the raise and stay where you are, there's a danger that your boss will bear a grudge. *The upside:* You don't *really* know how your boss will react until you've made your move. In a no-lose situation, you might as well try.

How to Use Your Ideas— And Those of Others— To Your Best Advantage

Ideas are the bread and butter of your career. Any executive worth his or her salt will have more than an average number of good ideas every day. Over the years, I have worked out the following system of generating ideas, and it can work for you:

Keep a small notebook or pad with you (a microcassette recorder will work just as well) at all times. The minute any idea occurs to you, record it—and never make any judgment about its merits or lack thereof. Review these raw ideas a day or two later, and apply your judgment only at that time.

I've found that some of the ideas that seemed great to me at their moment of conception looked skimpy when objectively reviewed later on. Conversely, I've also found that some ideas that seemed flawed by flamboyance, lack of scope, or other problems later proved to contain things of value.

The secret? Reserve judgment, and do some energetic thinking.

Giving Away Ideas

Once you're producing a large number of ideas, one of the best things you can do is to give them away. The ability to go to a colleague and say: "For what it's worth, here's a thought I had on that problem in your department. . ." brands you as a colleague who is cooperative and helpful— with such a productive mind that you don't need to cling to each idea as though it carried a personal copyright.

Don't overlook the political advantages of this process. It puts you in the position of deserving support from colleagues. It also gives you leeway to use their ideas— among other favors—to your benefit.

When you have a truly wonderful idea, enhance your proprietary control over it through documentation. Present it in memo form, with copies to all concerned.

If someone has appropriated an idea you haven't documented, and you're angry, try first to get back into the process by writing a memo: "Here are some further thoughts on the marketing plan I proposed. . ." If this fails, speaking to a member of upper management with whom you have firm political ties may be justified. But it is often better to reassert your clout by winning some key project or promotion, to show your colleague that you still have a power hand.

Using Other People's Ideas

I've spoken elsewhere in this book of crippling rules that inhibit success. One of the greatest of these is the notion that another person's idea is completely proprietary, and that he or she has the right to retaliate if you use it to your own advantage. This is simply not true. A few observations:

The idea that seems most valuable to you—the very solution to some major business problem—may actually be of little significance to the person who thought it up. In some cases, he or she may not even remember it.

A cooperative attitude—asking permission to use an idea and giving credit where it is due—is often the key to profiting from others' ideas. People are generally complimented if you are able to use their intelligence to your own advantage. They get to share the credit for something that worked well—and get someone else (you) to do all the sweating.

How to Distance Yourself from a Boss in Trouble

The easiest way is to observe this precaution: Shape your relationship with *any* boss in such a way that you are associated with him or her in all of the best professional ways—and in very few of the ways that will get you in trouble if hard times come.

A healthy relationship with a boss has the following characteristics:

- **Personal independence.** Don't always be seen with your boss—the "me and my shadow" syndrome. Resist the temptation to cultivate a close tie with your boss exclusively by socializing—be sure to earn his or her support through a *variety* of means.

- **Professional liberation.** In your relationship with your boss, be clear that your work activities are *your* products—even though you may have been instructed to produce them. To avoid being viewed as an extension of your superior, invest your work with your personal approach and content.

- **Political independence.** Develop a broad range of contacts and a network of support in which your boss is not the only player. Report to him or her, but interact with dozens of other key people.

If your boss falls into disfavor with top management, you must immediately decide whether or not that disfavor is justified. If your boss really has been performing inadequately, continuing to lend unqualified support will only make you more closely associated with your boss's team and less likely to survive any coming debacles.

If, on the other hand, your boss is genuinely capable and upper management is acting unfairly, you will have to weigh a variety of factors and plan your appropriate actions accordingly. Consider:

- **Upper management style.** If your company's leaders motivate workers by instilling fear, it's possible that your boss may not be on his or her way out. Bide your time, see what happens.

- **Your boss's clout.** If your boss is a well-respected person in your industry (your research should have determined this long before problems arose), it might be wise to continue your support. Your supervisor will land on his or her feet with some other company or emerge victorious from the current power struggle, and your support will have earned you gratitude and a shot at advancement. Even if your boss loses the struggle and leaves the company, the fact that you continued your support may not work against you with top management—especially if your boss landed in the doghouse because of a difference of style or approach rather than accusations of incompetence.

How to Get Twice as Much Done in Half as Much Time

There are a lot of books that will tell you how to use charts and schedules to manage your time more effectively. Go get one of them if you must, but first let me tell you how to get much more done in much less time than it takes to read a book:

- Whenever possible, use quick conversations instead of formal meetings.

- Avoid business lunches. Too often they are more lunch than business.

- Hire the best workers you can find and delegate as much work to them as you decently can.

- Don't just close your door when you're reprimanding somebody—close it for several hours every day to establish a pattern and use the time to work like mad when you have to.

- Answer letters and memos by writing an answer on the original and returning it rather than drafting a new memo. Keep a photocopy for your files.

- Get to the office early when you've got extra work to do. You'll get much more done before everyone arrives than you ever will by staying late.

- Set firm time limits on meetings. When people realize you *really* mean to end one-hour meetings after one hour, they'll hustle to cover their points quickly.

- Decide what to do with any document *the moment* you put your hand on it. Move it to an appropriate file or give it to somebody else to act upon.

- Have somebody else sort your mail. It sounds like a small idea, but setting priorities and having somebody else sort for you can free up more than *two hours* a week for more important projects.

4

Personal Patterns of Success

How to Bypass Your Firm's Salary Structure and Negotiate a 35% Raise

I've noticed that most people have no idea of how to gain rapid salary increases or rapid advancement. Yet there are simple approaches that can accomplish these things with surprising speed.

There's no one magic question that, when asked, will always make your firm start writing you much bigger checks. My experience has shown that seeking the kind of advancement we're talking about here rarely works for newcomers—you have to be ready, with your political network strongly in place.

How Not to Get Ahead Fast

Most people think in a *linear* fashion, believing that promotions will come as they move upward in a line from position to position. This system works, but slowly.

Other people have more developed theories on advancement, believing that throwing all their effort at building departmental profits, or something else, will gain the attention of upper management and result in their advancement. This system is really only a variation of linear thinking—and it's not much more effective.

The Key to Advancing Rapidly

In today's work climate, the key is to look outside your firm—even if you intend to remain there. Look at trends in your industry, look at how your firm is conforming to them—or failing to—and position yourself several steps ahead of the field.

The bottom line: Determine the position your company is going to need to have filled in six months or a year—and then *hire yourself for the job* before it is actually created.

Several years ago, I had the opportunity to see a young woman put this strategy into effect with remarkable results. Hired as a sales representative for a computer and office equipment company, she foresaw that more and more business users would be linking their computers together into local-area networks (LANs) within the next few years. She visited suppliers and learned all she could about LANs. When the market opened up—as she knew it would—she was already on top of the situation. And she was assertive enough to nail down the position of supervising the firm's network sales and customer support services, rather than just selling networks while somebody else took the job she had carved out for herself.

Like this woman, you'll have to be political enough to ensure that you're the person who will take the job you've created. But with thought and planning, the possibilities for advancement are tremendous.

- **New marketing strategies.** Is there some new marketing approach or tool that is well suited to your products or company goals? If so, become the in-house expert.

- **New markets.** It's not always easy to spearhead a company's expansion into a new market—particularly if you're in lower management. But if you think that some new product—or a variation of one already in production—could open up new profits, don't hesitate to educate yourself about the possibilities. Then, make a pitch to oversee the expansions.

- **New geographical areas.** If you know a lot about an area of the country—or even a foreign country—where your firm has not yet made inroads, you may have a golden opportunity at hand. Especially valuable: an insider's knowledge of a foreign country or fluency in a foreign language. (Note: Much of American business still remains phobic about foreign languages—you have a great opportunity to position yourself favorably if you know one.)

- **New joint ventures.** Consider the nature of your company's products or services, and the possible benefits of a joint venture with another business.

How to Know the Difference Between Jargon You Must Use and Jargon That Merely Stamps You as a Lightweight

Business generates new words and expressions almost every day. It's tempting to jump in and start spouting the latest lingo to show that you're on top of a trend. But using language the wrong way only makes you look like a faddist.

You'll do well to avoid the following:

- **Meaningless phrases.** A new expression isn't good just because it's new. Take an objective look at terminology and decide which words are *useful*. Is the new term *really* the clearest, simplest way to express a concept? If not, don't use it.

- **Jargon that excludes people.** Using a new word or acronym that half the people in the room have never heard before may make you feel stylish—but chances are you'll only be seen as impolite.

- **Words or expressions that you don't fully understand.** Misapplication of a word is a sure-fire way to look stupid.

- **Craze phrases.** Will people still be using the expression in six months? Remember when all the politicians were tripping over one another trying to use the phrase "Where's the beef?" every time they opened their mouths? Remember how stupid they sounded?

- **Overusing a word or phrase.** Don't become so enamored of a new phrase that you use it all the time. People will stop listening.

How to Decorate Your Office So That You Look Like a Leader

Your office should function well for *you*. It should look clean and efficient, without piles of paper or other clutter around. But you must also pay close attention to your office's atmosphere. Does it convey an air of seriousness and efficiency? Does it look like a place where some valuable thinking is taking place?

I have visited the offices of many important people in my day, and they all shared the qualities I mention above. Curiously, very few of them achieved the same results in the same way.

To decorate your office as a leader would, obey the following rules:

- **Express your personality.** Your office should reflect your interests and pursuits. Include things that appeal to you. Looking for items to please other people only waters down the personality you're trying to convey, and can make you seem wishy-washy. Never be ashamed of your tastes. If you love your classic 1967 Corvette, put a picture of it on the wall—even if your colleagues all have reproductions of Impressionist paintings.

■ **Include things you understand.** If you put up a painting or a framed quote you like and know about, you'll create a positive impression when you explain it to people. If you put up something you're supposed to like but really don't, you'll seem pretentious.

■ **Use help wisely.** As you climb the ladder, someone will offer to decorate your office. If you can keep your interests at the center of the plan, fine. Otherwise, refuse and keep your office the way *you* like it.

■ **Avoid the commonplace.** Don't decorate your space with two or three innocuous, framed posters that the mailroom brings you—it's another way to ensure anonymity. By the same token, avoid cute cartoons at all costs. Displaying a cartoon of a monkey saying: "I Hate Mondays!" will only make people view you as a monkey who hates to work.

What a Well-Positioned Mentor Can—And Cannot—Do for You

There has been a lot written about mentors over the last several years. A mentoring relationship is actually a close political alliance in which the flow of information goes more strongly in one direction than in the other. This usually occurs when a more senior person recognizes some special potential in a subordinate and singles him or her out for cultivation.

My own belief is that a broad network of cultivated

relationships is likely to be more beneficial to a younger manager than a strong political alliance with one senior person would be. However, if there is one powerful person who seems to take a special interest in you and wants to further your ideas—or who is very well placed and knowledgeable in your field—the advantages of cultivating a relationship may outweigh the lack of political mobility you'll have to accept.

You don't have to be crazy about somebody to want to establish a close alliance with and learn from him or her. Sometimes respect and an attitude of interest are all that are needed to form the backbone of a mentor-student relationship. But in most successful cases, the relationship has been nurtured and strengthened by political cultivation.

A well-placed mentor will speed your progress and, with luck, teach you some important things. However, you should be aware of the following pitfalls:

■ **Picking the wrong mentor.** In your eagerness to establish ties with a bigwig, don't establish ties with somebody who is not well connected, who doesn't know as much as you expected, or who is about to leave. Do your homework carefully before establishing ties. You're better off being unallied than tied to the wrong person or camp.

■ **Getting hamstrung.** When you have a mentor, you can worry too much about taking risks, out of fear that your actions will reflect badly on your ally. So you become an ineffectual clone who waits for suggestions of what to do. *Defense:* Try to find a mentor who encourages independent effort, and continue to act with autonomy in most of your projects.

- **Getting reined in.** You have an idea you think is terrific, and go ahead and propose it at a meeting. To your surprise, your mentor is furious because he or she wasn't consulted, or thinks it is a bad idea. *Problem:* When you agree to a mentoring relationship, you are also agreeing to a certain amount of control.

- **Political limitations.** Having a mentor not only cuts you off from having close ties to your mentor's opponents, it also creates disturbances with colleagues at your own level. How would you like to have a colleague who shares your rank and title, but who has the ear of top management while you do not? Of course, your colleagues are free to advance themselves politically, but you must calculate the risk of schisms among your co-workers.

- **Ugly surprises.** Just because your mentor tells you all about certain things doesn't mean he or she will tell you that you're getting bypassed for a promotion, or that a key assignment is going to somebody else. The biggest surprise of all is when your mentor leaves. Never forget that you are a subordinate, and there are limits on the information you'll receive.

- **Blurring of roles.** Always remember that your mentor is your superior. In almost all cases, it is unwise to confide that you are unhappy with your job, or that you are seeking a new one. Also try to avoid gossip, unless a mentor asks you for it specifically. *Example:* Your mentor asks: "What is the feeling among your colleagues about the new management development program?" In matters of joke telling, sharing personal information, and social interaction, always let your mentor take the lead in establishing guidelines. For example, never be the first to suggest that you have lunch.

■ **Burnout.** A close relationship can eventually degrade if you become a threat—or a mental burden—to the person who has taken you on. Be willing to distance yourself when necessary and don't overtax the relationship by asking for advice too often, or stopping by when you have nothing—or something minor—to discuss.

How to Make Points with a Boss Without Obviously Being on the Make

Your relationship with your boss is likely to be taken as a microcosm of your future with the company. If you manage it well, it is taken as a barometer of your potential in the firm. Here are some vital pointers for managing this all-important relationship effectively:

■ **Question your viewpoint.** If you think your boss is either beyond reproach or incapable of doing anything right, you have failed to make an accurate—or useful— assessment of his or her abilities. And you are not meeting his or her needs. Go back to square one and take an objective inventory of what he or she can do.

■ **Learn how to format information.** As a subordinate, one of your major duties will be to supply your boss with facts. Don't format the process the way *you* like it. Try to meet your boss's preferences. If he or she prefers a daily morning chat to a stack of memos, oblige that need.

■ **Understand his or her personality—and your own.** For the relationship to work effectively, you may have to subjugate your own style. To accomplish this, you will have to do some self-analyzing. If you're fun loving and your boss is glum, superimposing your style on the relationship can result in disaster.

■ **Learn when to make proposals—and when to keep quiet.** Especially in the early stages of a relationship, it is vital that you offer only your best, and most fully developed, ideas. Spattering your boss with a buckshot hail of suggestions in the hope that some will hit the mark brands you as someone who is right only two or three percent of the time.

■ **Anticipate pressures.** Pay attention to how and when your boss feels pressure most acutely. *Examples:* Is it when he or she is facing a meeting with a particular high-ranking person? Is it when he or she prepares reports? Try to throw your support at these areas first. Don't blindly believe that your priorities match those of your boss.

■ **Defend your boss.** Never gossip about your boss's

shortcomings—it's far too dangerous a game. If your boss has fallen on hard times with upper management, then you will have to make an appraisal of his or her situation and act accordingly. In all but the most extreme cases, defending your boss is your own best defense.

Test Your Promotability: Are You *Really* a Logical Candidate for a Move Upward?

Just because you're doing an efficient job of handling most of the facets of your career, don't assume that you're promotable. When you get passed over for a big promotion, you'll end up saying: "How could they do that when I motivated my staff so well?" or, "How could they do it when I just got my first invitation to the boss's executive barbecue?" To make it to the top, you've got to keep building up the areas where you're weakest.

Don't say I didn't warn you. Take the following test. Any areas in which you answer *no* can scuttle your chances, so start working on them now.

- Have I established a strong individual presence and profile?
- Are my speech and communication skills as strong as I can make them?
- Have I consistently supported colleagues, taken an interest in their projects, and helped them achieve results?

- Have I demonstrated a strong ability to confront and solve problems, or have I just skirted them?

- Have I demonstrated an ability to perform under pressure?

- Have I consistently completed management's priority assignments before my own?

- Have I completed projects that demonstrated my specific strengths and abilities?

- Have I defined my long-term objectives, and do I understand the role my current activities play in attaining them?

- Have I supported my superiors by cheerfully taking on work in difficult periods and offering good advice?

- Have I achieved a high degree of political clout that reinforces the strengths outlined above and seals the promotion?